LOSS ≠ LOST

MONICA SELLERS-JENKINS

It is our prayer and declaration that you would maintain a Spirit of Integrity concerning the knowledge shared with you in this book. Meaning, when using the information in this book publicly, you would give author proper recognition and acknowledgement for the knowledge, work, experience, research, and labor of development of this book.

No part of this book may be reproduced by mimeograph process or by another method of duplication unless expressed written permission has been granted by Monica Sellers-Jenkins.

Ecclesiastes 12:14

For God shall bring every work into judgment, with every secret thing, whether it be good, or whether it be evil.

First Edition: 2022
ISBN: 978-1-934905-12-8
Worldwide Kingdom Publishing
1911 Horger St.
Lincoln Pk, Michigan 48146
www.drcharisseelewis.com

Copyright (C) 2022 by Monica Sellers-Jenkins
All rights reserved.

DEDICATION

This book is dedicated to any mother who has suffered the loss of a child.

This book is also dedicated to anyone who has ever suffered the loss of a child. My prayer is that the loss of a love one does not have to equal the lost of your peace of mind.

SPECIAL THANKS

I thank God for giving me purpose and allowing me to write this book at the time of the pandemic. God made me promise to no longer procrastinate.

To my husband of 32 years, Melvin K. Jenkins thank you for always believing in me. Thank you for your encouragement and your wisdom as my lover, my pastor, and my friend.

To my mother, Jennie Gudger I saw you do it all. Thank you for showing me how to remain strong and focus on my purpose and my call. Thank you for raising me in the church and thank you for all your prayers.

To my daddy, the late Robert J. Sellers for showing me what a real man should look like. You have always gently pushed me to do right. You were my greatest cheerleader. I love and miss you.

To my darling children, the late Melvin Jr., Shuantaia, and Melveshia. Thank you for allowing me to raise you. I appreciate you all for every lesson I learned. I thank you for making me a better prayer warrior. To my neph-son Daylen, you are simply the best nephew in the world.

To my only grandchild, Zyaire you are my sunshine. You make Gana smile daily.

To my siblings, you taught me so much. It was through our relationships that gave me strength. Love you all.

To the Sanders Family , and the Sellers Family I appreciate and love you all.

To my spiritual mom, Dr. Wanda Davis, thank you for literally saving my life. Teaching me to voice what I felt and giving me the help I needed. I love you more than words can say.

To my GSD Church Family, thank you for believing in me.

To Dr. Charissee Lewis, my friend, my mentor, and my publisher, thank you for pushing me into my next.

To Bishop Don Shelby Jr. & First Lady Bonita Shelby and Michigan Southwest Fifth Jurisdiction, thank you.

FORWARD BY PASTOR MELVIN JENKINS

The Lord has blessed my wife for life, First Lady Monica Jenkins, with an insight into the spiritual realm. She is able to take the reality of life to be a blessing or some may say, a help to someone that is hurting. She will take you through details of our life at a time that felt so devastating; but God showed up. He showed us all things are possible with Him in control.

This book is timely because we are living in a time when parents are often left laying their children to rest. This is a parent's worst nightmare. Our children should bury us. My prayer is that you will be encouraged. God was with us through this storm; He will surely bring you through your storm. The simple truth is God had to have his hand in this; otherwise the story could not have been told the way it needed to be told.

I have the experience to have endured this test that was bestowed upon us. I applaud and celebrate Lady Monica for her courage, with the help of the Lord to tell this story. This will help the next mother, father, sister, brother, or any family member, or friend who has suffered a loss. I would recommend this book to all, especially to those that are grieving and the pain won't go away. This book will help ease the pain and give comfort.

Greater Shiloh Deliverance Ministries
Detroit, Michigan 48228
Pastor Melvin K. Jenkins
Administrative Assistant

INTRODUCTION

My love for basketball started in the 7th grade. The day I picked up a basketball I was oddly enough in control of the dribble. As I was introduced to the game, my love grew because of my favorite player, Earvin "Magic" Johnson. I would watch Magic play at Michigan State for hours. Basketball became my focus for the next two years.

While at school, I played ball during gym class. As I developed my skills, I decided I would play in high school. I was short, but I was very fast. I learned how to handle the basketball. My position was point guard. Playing point guard meant you had to know the floor. You needed to know where your team mates were at all times. You could not drop a sweet pass if you did not know where to throw the ball. Being a point guard is like being an orchestra leader or choir director, you are in charge of creating the melody. Running point you are required to execute the plan or the play, you must have a third eye. You are in charge of the tempo of the game. Your team depends on you. A great point guard is able to anticipate the next move. As I watched Magic play, I noticed how he finessed the court. This man could play every single position. I would literally watch him close his eyes and make the sweetest passes. I would often wonder how he would know his teammate would be there. I would ask myself, "If I would ever throw a pass like that?" I would ask God, "If you would drop dimes like that would I be able to catch them?" I made the freshman team in high school and started every game. This had truly become my passion! Because of my height, people would count me out; but that was actually my secret weapon, liken unto David in the Bible. You must be able to be in control. You must maintain your cool. You need control, consistency, and cool, the three c's. Every time you touch the ball a plan should be developed. You need rhythm to go up and down the court. Playing point guard did not mean you would score all the points, it meant you had to make sure your team scored. I would only play the one year, but the love would remain in my heart for the game.

After college, I was able to coach a recreational team. I coached boys 13 and 14 years old. This is where I learned the meaning of mentorship. They were rambunctious young men who were determined to win. They prepared me for the next chapter of my life; which was becoming a mother to my son.

TABLE OF CONTENTS

First Quarter
Denial

Second Quarter
Anger

Third Quarter
Bargaining

Fourth Quarter
Acceptance

Overtime
Where I am Now

TABLE OF CONTENT

First Quarter
- Daniel

Second Quarter
- Esther

Third Quarter
- Ezra

Fourth Quarter
- A of prayer

FIRST QUARTER

DENIAL

As the days near to the change of weather, I sit and wait for spring. Spring Break comes and my son was so excited, he was on his way to Miami, Florida. As always, he had to have one more thing before he could board his flight. My phone rang, it's Melvin telling me he needed a bluetooth. I was thinking to myself why does he need a bluetooth on vacation? Of course, I go and pick the bluetooth up and drop it off to him. He was gone for about a week. He told so many stories about his trip, how awesome it was. Along with his stories he brought back a cold. This cold he brought back was annoying but he continued to go to practice. I didn't think much about the cold, because it was March. Being March meant we made it past the month November. You see every November for the past 2 years, we received bad news.

Let's digress to November 2004. We were on our way going to the National Holy Convocation in Memphis, Tennessee. I was feeling the worst I had ever felt in my entire life. Why did I feel so bad? The test results were back, and it said, "Cancer." What do you mean? My son is only 19 years old! He can't possibly have cancer. He is the healthiest child I have, my basketball player. He has been hooping since middle school. The doctors said we must see an oncologist as soon as possible. As I sat at the convocation in pain, I wanted God to send me a word. All of these powerful anointed people around me and no one feels my agony. Service after service, I go in empty and I come out empty. I am thinking, why am I here? I felt overwhelmed not knowing what the future would hold. I asked God for three sons and only received one. God could not possibly be planning to take my one and only. God you instructed me to lay hands on barren women and they conceived. Not just conceived, but they conceived sons. This test is so unfair, I thought you loved me. It is not right, God please wake me up from this nightmare.

We returned to Michigan and went to the oncologist. He explained we were dealing with soft tissue Sarcoma. He told us we needed to see the surgeon next. How do you tell a ball player you need to cut off half of his foot? We went to get a second opinion with the same identical diagnosis. What happened to God healing the sick? My life just hit turbulence like I was on an aircraft.

After surgery, it was time for chemotherapy. They would place a port in his chest to filter the drugs through his body. These treatments would start at 7a.m. and last until about 4p.m. Prior to starting his monthly chemotherapy, I would have to give him shots in his stomach before each round. Melvin had grown his hair out, and by round two of chemo it had all fallen out. He would sleep the whole time during his treatment sessions, and I would read my word and pray. The nurses would come in and check on us periodically throughout the day. Each round would last three days. Eating was very hard for Melvin, his appetite had decreased tremendously. There was a Wendy's in the hospital, so I would go there to try to get him to eat chicken nuggets.

Day after day, we would sit in our private room doing whatever it was they told us to do. I knew God could heal through chemo. I would fast for days at a time. I knew God had the master plan. My husband the great Pastor that he is, continued to feed his congregation. I could not understand how he kept preaching. He never missed a Sunday. He had so much faith that God would heal. Yes! He would heal! I was determined to attend every treatment. After chemo and surgery, he would learn to walk again with a prosthetic.

He began to work out again and the gym became his best friend. Practice started up with the team. Not only did he need to learn how to walk, but he learned to run, too. Melvin did so well teaching himself to learn the game all over. Our entire family supported him in every aspect. The first game he played after the amputation was phenomenal! Once he got in the game, he hit a 3 point shot the crowd went wild. The opposing team did not know why everyone was so excited about that shot! That shot was more than 3 points! It meant God had returned him to his first love. It meant we had beat cancer. He played so well you couldn't tell he had a prosthetic foot. My husband and the entire family gave him a standing ovation.

Thanksgiving was his favorite holiday and this year we would celebrate big! All of our family and friends were here, what a wonderful time we ate and laughed all day. Melvin was so happy with everyone being here. The house was filled with happiness and joy, most of all peace. Only God could give you peace during a storm.

A year had gone by and no bad news. Right at the time we felt safe, like God had answered all of our prayers; but once again, we went to the doctor and they discovered a hernia. We thought it was because he was working out so hard; but the cancer was back. No way! How did this happen, again? Here we go needing surgery once more. This time he would have to go through radiation (*Where are you God*?). Once the hernia was removed he would be down again. He was not able to bounce back so quickly like the last time.

Most of the time, recovery is a state of mind. When people are ill they need peace in their mind. They need to know that God has not left them. There is an assurance needed that God is still a healer. They need to know that God is still the author and finisher of our faith. I am believing and trusting him no matter how long it takes. I will trust the Lord at all times with all my heart. I will not lean to my own understanding, even when I do not see progress.

Looking back, he loved basketball and would pick up a ball every chance he got. Now basketball was my game I thought I knew the game well. I was his first coach and I coached his little league team. He was not very good and was not very tall; but he had heart. Melvin practiced daily. We would often play two on two in the backyard with his friends. He would often tell his friends, "You cannot guard my mom." So funny this is how he first started protecting me. Right before he took his last breath he did the same thing, protected me!

I replay the last day over and over!

SECOND QUARTER

SECOND QUARTER

ANGER

I received a call from my husband at 7a.m. stating he wants to go to the hospital. I knew he had a scheduled appointment later that day. Why go early? I met my husband at his apartment and Melvin could not get out of the bed. My husband literally carried him down the stairs and put him in the car. To see his appearance, the drastic change, the muscles had deteriorated, and his weight was gone. He had to be down to 100 pounds. At the doctor's office they could not get a pulse. Wait! What's going on? Then I heard these words I will never forget. Dr. B turned to us and said, "The cancer is winning." I thought wait God, you are going to heal him. Did you forget about healing Melvin? Where are you? You had me lay hands on infertile women and they conceived sons. There is no way you would take my only son. I am constantly crying out to you, constantly asking for your help, and where are you? I have served you unconditionally, and this is the thanks I get?

As Dr. B stated the cancer was winning, he then asked the ultimate question. He asked, "Do you want to be resuscitated?" Melvin turned to his dad and looked at me and said, "What do you think?" The entire world stopped spinning at that very moment. My husband asked Melvin, "Are you afraid?" Melvin replied, "A little." Melvin asked, "Now what Dad?" You could literally hear a pin drop. I thought about all the times that I told him to have faith and trust God. I thought about the times when God would show me the occupation of all my children. I never saw the occupation to pray for Melvin. Was I supposed to know then that he wouldn't make it to see 23 years old? I told him to trust You, God. I told him You would never leave us, nor forsake us. This has become a huge lie. Where are you God?

Dr. B begin to tell us what would happen if they tried to resuscitate him. The look on Dr. B's face was blank. From here, we answered the question and said, "No!" Everyone in the room began to cry and I left the room. So much was going through my head. I had to contact my mom and my daughters. As I spoke with my mom, I had to admit I was angry with God. My oldest daughter was my next call. I had to figure out a way to get her home from college without telling her the entire story. I also needed to contact Melvin's girlfriend who was out of the country. I ran into Dr. B in the hall and he gave me the biggest hug ever, and told me if it was his son; he would make the same decision. His attempt to comfort me meant a lot, but where is the Comforter? Things escalated very quickly once they admitted him in the hospital. The word got out.

The final time he protected me. Nurses kept coming in asking questions. I asked the nurse could we speak in the hall. She complied and we stepped out of the room. I asked her if she could refrain from asking him how he felt. She said, "No problem." We went back in the room. She then proceeded with questions and went right back to asking him how he feels. Before I knew it, I told her you are not a very good listener. My husband then asked her to step out of the room, once again. I explained to her how would you feel if you were dying? I then proceeded to tell her do not ask him that question again! I did not return to the room, but my husband and the nurse did. My son said to her, "Please understand my mom, I'm her baby. So I apologize to you, if my mom said anything to threaten you!" Once I returned to the room, the nurse told me what my son had said. So many people were arriving at the hospital, they change his room twice to accommodate us. His basketball team and friends from elementary were all there. Our family and friends were there, as well. When my daughter arrived, you could see the disappointment in her eyes. They did everything together. She asked for everyone to leave the room, so she could have a private moment with her brother. At some point during the day, over 50 people had been there to visit him. They had conversations about old times, they talked basketball and now he was gone to sleep. I ran around the entire afternoon trying to make sure all those that were important to him were there. By the time I returned and settled down, he never opened his eyes again. Once his girlfriend's flight landed, she came straight to the hospital. She would spend time with him. One final scrimmage! After several hours, she left the hospital to go home to freshen up.

We sat there a few more hours and I clearly heard God say, "You have to let him go." I sat straight up and my friend stated, "You have to let him go!" So we all began to go to his bed; as I told him it was okay to leave. He opened his eyes, tears rolled down his cheeks. He winked one eye and took his last breath. Him always joking, he left even with a grin on his face. My "Little Melvin" as I affectionately called him, left this earth. I knew he would go after his girlfriend left, because he didn't want her to witness the final whistle of the play!

Anger is defined as a strong feeling of displeasure and belligerence; aroused by a wrong. With anger comes resentment and blame and those two can really change your insight and outlook on life. I needed a clear understanding from God, why I felt the way I did? You can become consumed with fury. Anger is normally targeted towards someone or something. Anger will take you into rooms you are not prepared for. Rooms like resentment, wrath, and blame. You will find fault in every decision you make once anger enters in. You tell yourself God doesn't love you. You can not hold on to anger and nurse it: because it will actually kill you. This can lead to high blood pressure. From that, you can develop kidney failure, and many other diseases. We must be conscious of how we allow anger to direct us. The best thing to do is to let the anger go. If we focus on what went wrong, we will never get pass it long enough to become healed. This is what the devil is banking on that we will never stop and ask God for deliverance. If the enemy can keep us in bondage, he wins. When you become so angry that you see red; you have lost a since of reality and that is when everything goes downhill. You honestly can not concentrate on anything but anger. You can not work. You can not care for your family. Drastic measures has to be taken when anger is ruling your life. Hurting people hurt other people. Some people hurt themselves by using substances, because they are trying to get a grip on anger. I have a one word solution to anger and it is, Jesus!

Some situations will cause you to have resentment. We can become resentful because other people seem to be moving on with their lives. When we are affected by anger, we become stuck. The only way to come out from under this cloud is deliverance.

Ephesians 4:26-27
Be ye angry and sin not; let not the sun go down upon your wrath.

Prayer Against Anger

Lord, I pray that anyone who has lost a loved one that You will heal their heart. I ask God that You will open their understanding and help put the pieces back together, again. I ask that You will destroy the strongholds that are preventing them to soar. I ask God that You will place people in their lives that will help them move forward from grief. God please comfort them when they are sad and lonely. Father, lift the heavy burden of faultfinding. Father, deliver them from the brokenness. The blood the Jesus Christ cover their thoughts and cleanse their hearts. Give them victory and peace. In Jesus Name. Amen.

THIRD QUARTER

BARGAINING

I prayed for three sons and I only wanted boys. I guess this was my comfort zone. I coached boys basketball and ministered to young men at team ranch. Boys were very easy for me to teach and train. Boys were very competitive and they always wanted to win. Pushing these young men was easy, because they always wanted to out do the next player. They wanted to out shine one another. When I would *demonstrate* a play for them it would make it easier for them to understand. I learned early on boys are visual. They learn by what they see. In my teen years, I saw three boys I would raise, but God didn't. As I picked names for boys, I was convinced that I would have three sons. One day sitting in the doctor's office, I prayed and asked God to deliver my only son from this horrible disease. I said to God, "Take me because my son has too much to live for; if there is anyway Lord can he stay?

Please tell me what to do. I know you love me and I know You love him; but can You allow him to stay? God, I don't wish this pain on any mother. Lord, did you get the children mixed up? Why not take a murderer?" Your scripture says, You were wounded for our transgressions and I know this disease is not too big for You! Lord, please don't take my only son.

The day he walked into my life everything changed. I thought You had forgotten about my requests for a son. I met this little boy when my husband and I began to date. Little Melvin, as I called him was such a quiet child. Two months after we said, "I do." There he was in the middle of the kitchen floor screaming, "Somebody help me!" As I entered into the kitchen, I realized he simply needed to know what to call me. As we were the only two in the home, somebody became "mommy". This moment was the beginning of our special relationship. The word "step" was not in our vocabulary. I was never "stepmom" and my husband was never "stepdad". In our household, we were both just mom and dad, to all of our children. We worked hard to show our children we loved them equally. There was never my kid, or your kid, only ours.

As Melvin grew older, as did our bond. No one would ever guess I hadn't carried him for nine months. We spent so much time together. I remember our first summer together. I prepared him for school, after I noticed he was behind. We worked on spelling, reading, and math. Melvin, affectionally was called "Jay" by most; but I called him, "Little Melvin". When he turned 13 years old, he asked me for a special gift. Something that I could only give him. He wanted me to stop asking him what he thought and felt about our relationship. His requests assured me, that he knew how much I loved him. It was my job to make sure that he knew my love was genuine, because my daughters were the children I birthed. I was determined that he would never feel unloved. My desire and goal was to make him feel loved and special. We were the team in our household. We were the Lakers and they were the Pistons. Of course, we were always out numbered; but we didn't care. We would take projects on in the house just for us to complete. One night we played hooky from Sunday night service just to paint. But of course, we had other motives, we painted very quickly. We really wanted to watch this movie. So our goal was to finish within the hour. We had popcorn we got to eat by ourselves, while the other 3 were gone. We met our goal and by the time they arrived home from church the movie was just ending. Most of the next several years was a breeze. The biggest thing that would happen with his health was once a year he caught a cold. He would become such a mama's boy when he didn't feel well. I would nurse him back to health with my soup and love. So why wouldn't it work now? I would continue to ask God this question over and over. Was I not prepared for the battle? Where did I drop the ball? How could you let this happen, Lord? I felt like Jesus when He was on the cross. When He asked God if this cup could be removed from him. After the diagnosis, we thought okay he can beat this. We had so much faith. I remember my spiritual mom saying God did heal him, but it was just not the way you thought. She then asked, "Is he in anymore pain?" I answered, "No!" Then she asked, "Is he suffering?" I answered, "No!" She then said, "He's healed!" I said, "Oooooo Chile!" That hit me like a ton of bricks and I finally got it! I had a light bulb moment. HE IS HEALED!

God had not forgotten me. His healing did not look like my expectations, but it was still a healing. Many times, we ask God for some things; but He does it differently than our expectations and we get angry. But God knows what's best for us. He knows what we need. He knows what we can handle, if we would just not complain about the situation and see it through God's eyes. Walk in His purpose and plans not your expectations. My purpose was to be a boy's mom of just, one. My purpose was to pour into him as long as I could. My purpose now is to pour into mothers who have lost a child. My purpose was to write this book and to let you know you don't have to be lost, because of loss. God still has a plan for your life. He has never given up on you or on your dreams. There is a plan for your life after the loss. You can't remain in neutral, you must get back in the driver's seat. Losing a loved one can make you feel lonely and sad. It can make you want to stay in park. The devil's job is to kill, steal, and to destroy. But if you keep reading, then it says "But I come that you may have life more abundantly." We must walk by faith and not by sight. What we see is momma left, daddy's gone; but see an opportunity for you to pursue Christ. Take a deep breath and push. You have something to birth. Get refocused and shake the dust off and move forward. Lift up your heads, ole ye gates and walk into your victory. Don't allow this hurt to consume you. Roll up your sleeves and fight, your sanity is worth fighting for. If you can't swim then float; just don't drown. Don't allow your sorrows to dictate your future. There is life after grief. You will advance if you ask God for peace and praise. Trust God and praise your way into peace.

FOURTH QUARTER

FOURTH QUARTER

ACCEPTANCE

Acceptance is the act of taking or receiving something that is offered. It is extremely hard to accept the death of a loved one, specifically speaking, the death of a child. It affects every part of your being; spiritually, mentally, emotionally, physically, and financially. It was so challenging losing my son. I don't know how one can make it; especially if God is not the center of your joy. No one wants to feel the anguish of losing a love one. The overwhelming sense of loss and loneliness can cause depression. This road leads to gloom and darkness if you do not allow God to come in and take control. Consequently, acceptance is the action or process of being received as adequate or suitable. Acceptance is needed in order to get to the final step in understanding that Loss does not equal Lost.

One week prior to my son's death, unfortunately, the Lord clearly showed me a funeral procession. I immediately began to cry and asked the Lord, "Do I have this wrong?" I then said, "God please tell me it's not what I think!" Well, it was God showing me my son was about to transition. I will never forget, we were in route to go and visit him as God decided to share this. I couldn't even get out of the car to go into the house. As God began to prepare me, there was an overwhelming feeling of disappointment. I felt like God had given up and I felt like there was no fight left within me. I began to feel doubtful and defeated. For the next hour I tried to pull myself together. I went in to visit my son, finally. Little Melvin could tell I had been crying. He asked, "If I was alright," and of course I said, "Yes I'm good." I began to ask him questions, because of what God had just shown me. The first question I asked, "What's your favorite color?" He replied, "Purple!" I am reminded in the vision he wore a purple tie. It had become clear to me that everything that God had shown me was how my son wanted it. I remembered when he went to prom; he wore purple and white. So everything now will be about those two colors. Holding back tears, we continued our conversation. It was four days later, my only son would take his last breath. I had to accept God's will. This was the Lord's will for him to enter into eternity. Sometimes, His will does not look the way we want it to look. We must have faith continuously, that grain of a mustard seed faith. Faith that sees, the impossible and that's how we overcome. We must trust the Lord with all our heart and not lean to our own understanding. There is a song that says, accept what God allows, and that's now my testimony. God has a way of getting us to focus. Every obstacle that gets in our way it helps us to learn to trust God. Every decision God makes won't be easy to accept, because His thoughts are not our thoughts and His ways are not our ways. Coming to terms with God's decisions sometimes takes a while. However, God does not make mistakes. God's timing is not our timing; but one thing for sure is, His timing is perfect. During the grieving process, we often think tomorrow it will all be over; but the truth is it's never over, grieving never stops. The good news is God teaches you how to grieve and live through it. It has been fourteen years, and some nights I still cry myself to sleep. The difference between year one and year fourteen, is the grace of God. Now I am aware of how not to get lost in my grief. See the pain is the same; but I no longer allow the enemy to drown me in the grief. His grace is sufficient for me. I now understand that becoming lost will defeat the purpose that God intended for me to learn. I am more determined to grow through the grief. This pain turned my purpose into helping other mothers who think they can't continue to live. I decree and declare that you can and will make it! I am asking God to hold you close as you read these words. You may have some bad days, but keep moving, those tears you cry are just cleansing your soul. Keep pushing to see the sun through the clouds. As you focus on your purpose, it helps give you strength to endure the hard days. Birthdays and the anniversary of your love one's death are the hardest days. During those times, plan things with your family and celebrate that love one. Some events are hard to attend like a wedding of your child's friend. You will wonder how their wedding would have been. You will even have days wondering what type of parent your child would have been; but with all of that, continue to focus on the memories. There are times that I ask God to just let me dream of him. So we can have that last conversation. I know our love ones would want us to be happy and have peace. The heaviness sometimes will hit and it seems as the earth is shattering. Take a deep breath and know that God is with you. Do not try to push the pain away, just allow it to run its course. Know that God won't put more on you than you can bear. It's like being in the forth quarter with 20 seconds left on the clock and your team is behind by two points. You can't win unless you hit a 3 pointer. You have to set a pick, and isolate yourself, and shoot! In the clutch, with seconds dwindling, release the shot. Swish, game time!

We always win no matter how hard it gets. Never leave the court before the clock hits zero. Be consistent in believing God even through the test. If you become fearful during the test, stop and ask God for clarity. Now, it may take years to become comfortable in moving on; but it is a must. We can not allow the devil to hold us in a holding pattern like a plane not given clearance to land. Be determined to heal. Be determined to reach your full potential. I am so grateful to God for ushering me into the place of acceptance. So many times God trust us with a trial just for us to grow. I pray whatever your loss is whether it's the death of a love one, a divorce, or the loss of a job; you will move again. I pray that you will gain strength and focus to prosper. It does not matter what the score board may say, "We always win!"

OVERTIME

OVERTIME

Now is not the time to be afraid. After my son passed, I became over protective with the two daughters I had left. This is how fear sets in, we can not live in fear. We can't stop living either. We can not live with doubt; we must hold fast to the promises of God. Everything God has planned for us we must stay focused and motivated. Do not stand still no matter who comes or goes keep it moving. Some people can not walk with you through the duration of your metamorphous. Once there is a loss of a love one, you change. There are several stages you go through; but there is a process you must complete. In the last 14 years, my process has been a roller coaster. At the end of the day, I learned how to process every stage of grief. Most importantly, I learned how to turn the pain into purpose. Writing my book was therapy for me and I learned the bond between a mother and son can never be broken, not even by death. I will forever love and cherish every memory of my son. I now understand that the Loss does not equal Lost. I cry some days, but it is not hopeless. There is a time to mourn and it is okay to be sad; just don't remain sad. You are not a bad parent if you live and be happy. Your child would want you to live a prosperous life. Your time is so important, you can never regain time, utilize it wisely.

Getting out of the bed after the funeral was probably the hardest day ever. Now everything was finalized so I didn't know what to do. I thought to myself maybe it was a bad dream. Not being a person who sleeps very well, I would just lay in bed awake. As I laid there, God began to download my next. I continued to lay there rehearsing the last week. I took calls, wrote thank you cards, and pushed passed how I felt. In the first several months after the funeral, I made sure everyone else was alright. I went into overdrive assuring that everyone else was taken care of. I continued to pour into others; while I was really on "E". It is very important after a loss you take care of yourself. Your peace is imperative for your sanity. When on an aircraft the flight attendant tells you if there is a need for oxygen put on your mask first. You can not help anyone if you are dead. It took me two years to understand, I must help myself first. Just as God showed me I was stuck; the answer came by way of a conference. This conference literally saved my life, and by the way, I thought I was fine. But I was not. During this conference, I realized I blamed myself for my son's death. In the back of my mind, I felt I should have done more. The healing that I needed met me in Atlanta, Georgia in a conference room filled with approximately 25 women of which all were strangers, except one. The next two days were filled with healing and deliverance and changed my life! I was angry at God and I didn't realize it. I had given up on being happy and I had no clue. By the time I left there, I had hope and a new lease on life. God showed me that I would become a bridge for those grieving. I have since developed a grief group which meets monthly to reach those who need help overcoming the hurdles of grief. We have had a 3 on 3 tournament, raising funds for cancer in my son's honor. I finally wrote this book which is intended to help mothers and others live again. My goal is to help parents to have a reason to get up and live.

PRAYER FOR THOSE HURTING FROM LOSS

Lord, I thank You for every person who picked up this book and read it. I ask that those hurting from loss that You would comfort them. Father God, we cancel every assignment of the enemy that makes them feel like they can't go on. I ask that You cover their hearts and their minds. We speak peace in their spirits, and ask that You give them a fresh wind. Let them be consumed with Your peace. We thank You for the victory, and they will get up and live again, in Jesus Name. Amen.

Ecclesiastes 3:1-8

There is a time for everything, and a season for every activity under the heavens: a time to be born and a time to die, a time to plant and a time to uproot, a time to kill and a time to heal, a time to tear down and a time to build, a time to weep and a time to laugh, a time mourn and

a time at to dance, a time to scatter stones and a time to gather them, a time to embrace and a time to refrain from embracing, a time to search and a time to give up, a time to keep and a time to throw away, a time to tear and a time to mend, a time to be silent and a time to speak, a time to love and a time to hate, a time for war and a time for peace.

Please repeat this if you would like to give your life to Christ.

Gracious Father, please forgive me for my sins that I know of and those I do not know of. Create in me a clean heart and renew a right spirit within me. I believe that Jesus Christ died for my sins and You now live in me. Teach me Your will for my life, so that I can live for You for the rest of my life. I gratefully receive salvation and ask that You continue to work on me. Thank You for saving me from all my sins. Amen. Now I ask that God will lead you to a Bible teaching church.

About the Author:

Affectionately known as Lady J, she is the sustaining force standing in the gap for her husband, Pastor Melvin Jenkins at Greater Shiloh Deliverance Ministries.
As the director of the Women's Ministry and an outreach minister for youth for over 22 years, she is an awesome teacher, life coach, marriage counselor, and advocate for children. Like the lilies of the field, her influence and appreciation from her community grows. Monica is committed to teaching young women life skills and how to be sufficient. Always leading by example, she was a foster parent for over 12 years. She has been married to the love of her life for 32 years. She is a devoted wife, the mother of two wonderful daughters, one son, two fantastic son-in-laws, and one grandson.

To contact the author:

If you would like to invite First Lady Monica Jenkins to speak at your church or event, contact her via email gsdladyj@gmail.com or by phone at (313) 909-2699. Thank you so much for expressing your interest to have Lady Jenkins speak at your event.

If you would like to attend Monica's grief group they meet the fourth Friday monthly on Zoom. Zoom code 4543736178

www.ingramcontent.com/pod-product-compliance
Lightning Source LLC
Chambersburg PA
CBHW071230160426
43196CB00012B/2468